Going Bananas!
A Kid's Guide To Puerto Limon, Costa Rica

Photography by John D. Weigand
Poetry by Penelope Dyan

Bellissima Publishing, LLC
Jamul, California
www.bellissimapublishing.com

Copyright © 2019 by Penny D. Weigand & John D. Weigand

All rights reserved. No part of this book may be reproduced or transmitted in any form or by any means, electronic or mechanical, including photocopying, recording, or by any other means, or by any information or storage retrieval system, without permission from the publisher.

ISBN 978-1-61477-381-8
First Edition

"It's always fun to go bananas!"

PENELOPE DYAN

Going Bananas!
Bellissima Publishing, LLC

Introduction

Puerto Limon, one of the most picturesque places in Costa Rica, sits right between Nicaragua and Panama, with lots of coconut trees, and (of course) bananas! And if you are lucky, you might see a monkey; and you might even see even a sloth hanging from or in a tree! Famous for bananas, if you happen to go on a guided tour of the region, you will hear all about the history of bananas in this region; and you may even get to taste a banana ripened by Limon's tropical sun! So, if you are going to go bananas, or if you decide to even go for bananas, (or perhaps anther tropical fruit) this is the perfect place for you to be! The people are friendly, and the dress is almost always casual! After all, you are only a hop, skip and a jump away from the beach, so even if Mom and Dad dress up to go out at night, chances are you won't have to put on anything to wear except for your swimsuit, or shorts and a t-shirt, or a sundress (if you are a girl, of course).

This is a fun, 'learn to read' book filled with word repetition, word recognition and rhyme, written by award winning author, attorney and former teacher, Penelope Dyan; and it is meant to give you a kid's eye glimpse of Puerto Limon. There is also a free music video that goes with this book you can find on Bellissimavideo's YouTube channel.

Going Bananas!
Bellissima Publishing, LLC

Going Bananas!
A Kid's Guide To Puerto Limon, Costa Rica

Photography by John D. Weigand
Poetry by Penelope Dyan

Mom says that there are a lot
of things in Puerto Limon to see,
and if you are VERY lucky,
you might EVEN see a MONKEY
hiding high up in a tree!

Bananas hang from trees here,
sometimes ripening in blue plastic bags;
AND what's more,
you can ALSO buy bananas
(just like THESE bananas)
from a fruit stand,
OR from a local store!

There's A LOT of fruit here
that YOU can buy AND eat,
fruit that is delicious AND ripe,
fruit that is oh so very SWEET!

Mom tells you to look up high
into a tree that NEARLY touches
the blue of the Caribbean sky!
And then lo and behold!
What is it that you SEE?
YOU see a Caribbean monkey
hiding HIGH up in that TREE!

In a store,
your mom buys a toy sloth for YOU!
AND she ALSO buys a toy sloth
for your SISTER,
because of toy sloths
(in this store)
there just happen to be TWO!

You find a golden mermaid
not so VERY far from the sea.
You wonder about the pirates of old,
and about the things of the future
that just MIGHT be!

You walk right down to the beach.
You see, it is VERY close!
AND it is NOT too hard to REACH!
And as you gaze out at the water,
you wonder how AND why . . .
the blue of Puerto Limon's
Caribbean water
seems to touch
the blue of Puerto Limon's
Caribbean sky!

Your mom buys your SISTER
a toy parrot.
And THEN Dad buys YOU a ball!
They have to reach up
to get them down from the shelf,
because you and Sis
just aren't very TALL!

You pass right by a nearby lagoon, and mom sadly tells you, "We'll be leaving here soon!"

Then you make one MORE stop,
and DAD complains,
because MOM wants (again) to shop!
Your sister gets excited.
Dad asks,
"Why ALL the fuss?"
And Mom buys you AND your sister
(each) a brightly colored toy bus!

Mom tries to convince you
this is a ONLY a chocolate treat,
but this is something that looks ICKY,
AND so (of this) YOU refuse to eat!
The man at the counter tells you
there are cocoa beans inside,
as behind your mother's skirt
you desperately TRY to HIDE!
Your sister decides it is ONLY right,
that she NOT try it
unless YOU first take a bite!

As the sun sets upon the sea,
a brand new adventure lies ahead.
AND you think about THIS,
as your mother tucks you into bed.
You think about the setting sun
and its reflection on the sea.
AND you think about that monkey
you saw so high up in that TREE!
And when you finally
close your eyes to sleep,
you think about
that beautiful golden mermaid . . .
and about
the silent creatures of the deep.

"*Every day of your life is a new adventure!
And this is how it should be!*"

PENELOPE DYAN

www.ingramcontent.com/pod-product-compliance
Ingram Content Group UK Ltd.
Pitfield, Milton Keynes, MK11 3LW, UK
UKHW060206250426

12048UKWH00053B/16